Quintessential Leadership Practically Applied

By

Sandra Ross

Copyright © 2014

Table of Contents

Preface

What is quintessential leadership? What does it look like? How do we, as leaders, apply it to and in our everyday lives?

This book gives a glimpse of what practically applying quintessential leadership in every aspect of our lives looks like.

The scenarios are diverse, but you'll see that quintessential leadership is more than just a to-do list in a limited scope or context. Instead, it is who we are, how we think, what we say, what we do 24/7.

There is no part of lives that quintessential leadership doesn't touch. My hope is that this book will be a springboard that gets you thinking about how to apply quintessential leadership - each application makes quintessential leadership a part of who and what you are - to your lives. Everywhere. In every way. In every thing.

Please subscribe to my blog, *The Quintessential Leader* (http://quintessentialldr.com), for more information on what quintessential leadership looks like.

Chapter 1: A Matter of Conscience

Conscience

I heard an excellent sermon on the role of conscience - what it is, why it is, and what it's supposed to do practically when guided by overarching moral principles of right and wrong (these are not self-determined, but determined by God and His word, which is, as <u>John 17:17</u> says in recording the prayer Christ prayed before going out to Gethsemane to face His executioners, truth).

It coincided with <u>a conscience-driven blog post</u> I'd written a few days prior and I realized that, sadly, at least in this particular area, I may be only one of a small handful on the planet with a fully-awakened conscience in terms of the big picture of right and wrong in this matter and the only morally-correct response an awakened conscience could have to it.

It seems the more I strive to practice and be a quintessential leader in every aspect of my life, the more I am aware of how much conscience plays a role in whether we are quintessential leaders or not.

It also seems that the human race, for the most part, has no collective or individual conscience at all. There is nothing bigger than themselves to which they are accountable or answerable.

There is no internal compass - which the conscience should be - that prods them to continual scrutiny of - and immediate action to change when they are wrong - their attitudes, their thinking, their motives, their words, their actions, who they are and what they think, say, and do.

I have become increasingly aware that quintessential leaders are few and far between in the human population. And those of us who are undertaking the quest to become quintessential leaders are, in our little corners of the planet, standing all alone. It shouldn't be that way, but that's the reality.

I also have come to realize that most people simply don't want to know - and for the most part, really don't care - what's wrong, and those who do often just don't want to change it.

Why? Because change is a 24/7 process that requires constant action. It also demands total conviction, total commitment, and unwavering perseverance. And it often involves loss, sacrifice and pain.

It also means standing all alone to do the right thing at times. And that takes courage. And it takes a conscience that is highly-sensitive to absolute truth and absolute right and wrong and discerns that wherever it occurs in life and responds to it.

Quintessential leaders have well-developed and highly-sensitive consciences. Encountering wrong internally or externally produces a strong and impossible-to-ignore (it can even be mentally and physically painful) reaction that forces us to make a choice to accept the wrong or reject the wrong.

However, unlike quintessential leaders, most humans don't like being "different" from everyone else. They also work very hard to avoid isolation because of principles (meaning they would rather compromise on many things that they should not than lose face or lose friends or lose companionship).

This tendency, however, has a huge cost. Choosing to go along with and remain part of the crowd means sacrificing the sensitivity of their consciences. Repeatedly doing this eventually sedates the conscience until there is no longer a reaction at all.

The challenge is to ask you - yes, you who are reading this - to stop what you're doing in all your ADHD busyness right now and spend some quality time with yourself to examine the state of your conscience.

Here are some questions to ask.

Do I have an awareness of my conscience, or have I lulled it to sleep by ignoring it over and over again?

Do I care enough about what is right and wrong to dare to and have the courage to stand alone among my peers and friends when my conscience convicts me, or would I rather compromise and have the approval of others?

Do I avoid having my conscience nudged or awakened because I'm content with the status quo of my life and I don't want to have to change anything or possibly experience loss, sacrifice, and pain?

Do I get angry at and reject anything that prods and provokes me to use my conscience to look at what I do, what I say, what I think, and what I believe because I've convinced myself that I'm right all the time and I'm not going to even consider anything other than what I say, think, and believe?

Do I purposefully ignore and avoid anything and everything that might make me have to use my conscience and make different choices in my life?

Has my conscience been sedated to the point that I don't have any real strong convictions about anything in my life, but instead will compromise on just about everything because that's what everyone else is doing?

These are just a few of the questions that we, as quintessential leaders, should be asking ourselves all the time.

The bottom-line question, then, is one that only you can answer for you and I can answer for me, "Am I a quintessential leader or am I an unquintessential leader?"

Quintessential leaders are characterized by taking action, endeavoring with perseverance, and moving forward toward the goal, the ideal. Unquintessential leaders are characterized by taking no action, making little or no effort, and, at best, no movement toward, and, at worst, backward movement away from the goal, the ideal.

All of us are one or the other. If we're not one, then we are the other.

I know which one I am, while not there in totality yet, working toward and going to be when it's all said and done.

Do you know which one you are? How does that answer affect your life from this moment on? Or does it even matter to you?

If it doesn't matter to you at all, then it's time to do some realignment. If it does matter to you, then how are we doing?

Chapter 2: Avoiding the Snake Oil Trap

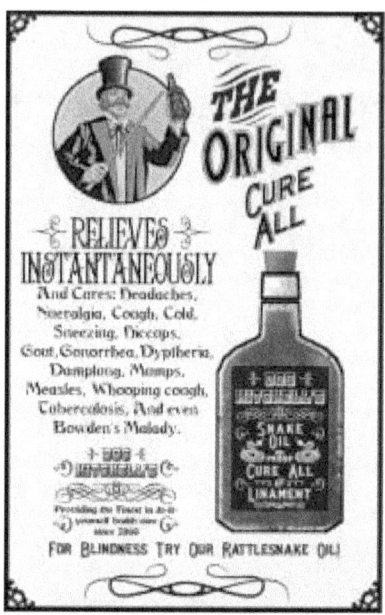

I hate <u>infomercials</u>. Not that I've ever watched more than about 10 seconds of any single one, but it was enough time for me to see that these are the modern equivalents of <u>snake oil</u>.

While the phrase *snake oil* originally referred to "medicinal" concoctions that included oil from snakes accompanied by outrageous claims of being magical curealls for every physical ailment in the world, the use of the phrase has evolved to refer to anything that is faddish, fraudulent, unsubstantiated, and promises a comprehensive and instantaneous one-shot-fix for everything.

While modern snake oil salespeople used to be confined to late-night cable TV, the advent of daytime talk shows (featuring celebrity gurus), the internet and social media has broadened their scope and base of people to dupe. They are literally everywhere and all us are bombarded with them everywhere we turn. It's enough to drive a sane person mad.

The snake oil formula is pretty simple. Create a recognizable salesperson and give him or her expert credentials (doctor, chef, wellness expert, financial expert, fitness expert, etc.) and elevate that person to demagogue status (if "X" or "Y" says it, then it must be true). Saturate people with their pitches. Get a lot of positive and glowing testimonials about whatever is being promoted. Laugh all the way to the bank. Oh, and sweeten the pot - and the profits - by creating pyramid selling channels to get your devotees to advertise and sell the product and give them a monetary incentive to do so.

Let's face it. We humans tend to be a pretty gullible lot. We also are very susceptible to promises of little effort, quick-one-size-fits-all-solutions, and great benefits instantly. There is something hardwired in our natures that make us gravitate toward snake oil solutions.

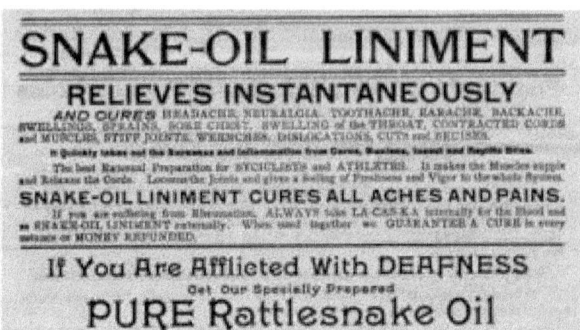

This susceptibility, though, can make us unwittingly blind (or willingly refusing to comprehensively research and prove or disprove the veracity) to outright deceit, inexcusable ignorance, twisting facts, limiting facts, angling facts, manipulating facts, omitting facts that snake oil promoters are masters at doing. Snake oil salespeople are the ultimate spin doctors and the human race is their all-too-willing victim.

I'll give an example I saw recently.

As well as being a quintessential leader passionately committed to developing quintessential leaders, I am also, because of extensive first-hand experience with my mom, a committed and passionate researcher, educator, counselor, author and blogger about dementias and Alzheimer's Disease.

I have been involved in exhaustive research about these neurological diseases for several years, first because I needed to get through all the misinformation and ignorance out there to be the maximum help to my mom with her specific dementias diagnoses (multi-infarct dementia, Lewy Body dementia, and Alzheimer's Disease), and now because I see the misinformation and ignorance largely continued. In this area of disease, there are tons of snake oil premises and solutions.

One of my primary missions is to reveal them for what they are and counter with *all* the facts. It doesn't always get me kudos because we humans desperately want that silver bullet that will solve everything at once and anyone who says there is no silver bullet and backs it up with exhaustive research and facts rains on the silver bullet parade.

So I was quite dismayed to see this article that continues the ignorant claim that Lyme Disease causes Alzheimer's Disease. That is patently untrue and the person who wrote this article, if he or she is a doctor, could have easily found that information.

How do I know this? Because I've written comprehensively about Alzheimer's Disease and its neurological genesis and physiological, behavioral, and mental manifestations.

In summary, here's my response to this snake oil claim. Alzheimer's Disease is a type of dementia. Not all dementias are Alzheimer's Disease. _Infectious dementia_ can be an advanced/late-stage outcome in a minority (10 to 15 percent) of Lyme Disease patients, but it _is not_ Alzheimer's Disease.

Does that seem overly picky to us? Are we thinking that it's all about the same thing, so why should it matter? If that's our reaction, then we're snake oil adherents.

Because truth matters. Precision matters. Complete and comprehensive education, knowledge, and understanding matters.

Without these, we, as quintessential leaders, will unconsciously or knowingly fall into the snake oil trap of always promising quick fixes, fad solutions, and instantaneous relief to complex, multifaceted issues and problems that will end in failure and disaster.

And the real casualty of the snake oil trap is trust and trustworthiness, a must have for all quintessential leaders. Once people don't trust us and we have proven ourselves to be untrustworthy, we are no longer quintessential leaders.

In fact, we're not leaders at all. We are mere pretenders standing at the back of a long line of snake oil promoters and salespeople who have preceded us.

Is that what we want our legacy to be? I'm convinced it's not.

Today I urge us all, as I join you because I do this continuously in my own life, to examine our lives, our thinking, our leadership principles, and our leadership toolboxes to see if we have allowed snake oil traps to creep into the way we do things and who we are.

If we have - and we are all so susceptible to this - then today is the day to get rid of them. Diligent education, knowledge, and understanding and vigilant care, watchfulness, and awareness - of ourselves and about everything else in our lives - are the keys to both avoiding and eliminating the snake oil trap.

How are we doing?

Chapter 3: Putting <u>and</u> Keeping First Things First

Most, if not all, organizations have an expressed mission statement. This should encapsulate why the organization exists and what its ultimate goal is. An organization's mission statement should always be the impetus for why the organization does what it does.

However, most organizations expend a lot of time, effort, and money on things that have nothing to do with their expressed mission statements. It's as though they needed to put something on a business plan, but it was just that - something on a business plan.

In other words, most organizations, at times throughout their existence, don't put *and* keep first things first. This is unquintessential leadership because it represents a loss of focus and vision.

And this is difficult for most organizations and the people they have in leadership positions to realize and see.

Why?

Because usually the replacement focus, goal, or project is a dependant subset of *the* priority (the technical writer in me needs to remind us that there is no such thing as *priorities*, because the word "priority" means "first thing," and there can be only *one first thing*) that is explicitly stated or implicitly understood in the mission statement.

We all, at times, tend to wander in our focus in this way. We tell ourselves that we're still focused on the priority because we're focused on a singular aspect related to *the* priority. But we are lying to ourselves.

Without *the* priority being continually rehearsed, reviewed, and maintained as what must come before *and* be the integral part of everything else we do, we lose sight of it, until it eventually disappears altogether, and we spend a lot of time, effort and money chasing our tails.

Quintessential leaders always put *and* keep first things first. Because *the* priority is always at the forefront of their thinking, their words, their actions, and indeed who and what they are, it is always the expressed starting point of everything else.

Why?

Because expressing *the* priority, whether spoken or written, each time reminds us and reminds our teams what is most important, why we are doing what we are doing, and that everything we do must be done within context of *the* priority.

Making *the* priority the expressed starting point of everything else also reminds us of what our focus should be and what our vision is.

Once focus and vision is lost because dependent subsets of *the* priority replace and eventually obscure *the* priority, then we are lost. Organizationally. Individually.

And when we are lost, it's often a long, long time before we realize it (if we realize it), and by the time we realize it (if we realize it), it's a long and arduous road back.

If we never realize we're lost, then we just become more lost. Ultimately, this is a fatal blow. Organizationally. Individually.

So I have several questions, my fellow quintessential leaders, that I want each of us to look in the mirror and ask of and answer for ourselves, not just today, but on a daily basis.

This is not a one-minute exercise. It requires digging deep in self-examination and it requires us being truthful and honest with ourselves.

That's what quintessential leaders do. Unquintessential leaders don't: they'll give this post a cursory glance (if even that), tell themselves "Of course, I do!" without a second thought and go on or they will ignore it altogether.

1. Are we putting *and* keeping first things first?
2. Do we remember what *the* priority is?
3. Do we make it an expressed statement of everything else, showing that it is what everything else depends on?
4. Have we drifted and lost focus of *the* priority?
5. Are we lost? If so, how do we get back?

If we find answers that aren't what we expected, what are we going to do?

The choice lies with each of us. Be sure it's the right one.

Chapter 4: The Priceless Value of Regular Quiet Time

As someone who craves and needs regular quiet time, I was surprised to read Matthew Hutson's underline article in *The Atlantic* last week discussing a new study that found that many people preferred electric shocks to being alone with their own thoughts. Having been shocked rather violently by electricity a couple of times in my life, I find it hard to imagine anyone would choose that over being alone with his or her thoughts, or, in other words, quiet time.

Quintessential leaders understand the value of quiet time and they use it regularly to regroup, reground, and recharge themselves.

We live in a world that is full of noise and activity. The more noise and the more activity we are exposed to, the less focused and thoughtful - in the sense of critical thinking - we become. Many people seem to prefer this frenzy of noise and activity, actively seeking it out and immersing themselves in it at every available opportunity.

The problem, though, without regular quiet time, is that constant immersion in noise and activity leads to the inability to know where the noise and the activity end and we begin. We lose ourselves at the very core of who we are, what we are, where we're heading, and what we believe. We become like shifting sand, drifting aimlessly from one thing to another, depending on the noise and activity we're surrounded by.

If we have the ability to think - some people have never used and developed this - we surrender that ability and our lives to the noise and activity of the moment. This is a very dangerous place for any of us to be because without the ability to think and regular use of that ability, we become impotent. And we become sitting ducks to be picked off by the charmers, the schemers, the seducers, and all the other gamers that exist in the world.

Regular quiet time is the anecdote to this threat. It is one of the most important and powerful tools available to each of us. But we have the responsibility to make it an integral part of lives and not let anything delay or remove it completely.

That takes desire, commitment, discipline, and active participation on our parts. It means saying "no" sometimes. It means turning off the noise and activity, the distractions that subvert quiet time, including unplugging from all the gadgets and devices that have made 24/7 noise and activity not only attractive, but seemingly an absolute necessity.

Here's a secret that quintessential leaders know: no human is so important and so necessary that any of us needs to be plugged in 24/7. In fact, we've found that being plugged in all the time makes us less effective, less productive, and less efficient. To believe otherwise is the epitome of egotism, arrogance, and narcissism - all traits of unquintessential leaders.

So how and why do quintessential leaders regularly use quiet time?

Quintessential leaders use quiet time to regroup.

I doubt anyone reading this doesn't have times when so much information - sometimes random, sometimes contradictory, sometimes unexpected - is coming at us at once that it's impossible to make sense of it, sort through it, and keep what we need and discard what we don't. (I have discovered over the years that my brain has a threshold where the door is bolted and locked and nothing else comes in after a certain point, so generally in large group and/or social situations, the longer I'm involved, the safer the information being given is with me, because I simply don't remember anything said after I hit my threshold.)

The result is a chaotic brain and action paralysis. Quiet time gives us time to think about, to process, and to give order to our thoughts. The interesting thing about quiet time is that is also gives us perspective, a key factor in regrouping.

We can literally sort through all the information, determining the credibility of the source, the validity of the information, and whether it's important and relevant to us, our lives, our teams, our goals. If anything doesn't match our sorting criteria, we can eliminate it. And what we're left with is the information that promotes taking action that will move everything forward.

If someone who's in a leadership position is action-adverse and/or never seems to be able to come to a final decision on anything, he or she does not have quiet time anywhere in his or her life.

Quintessential leaders use quiet time to reground themselves. The stuff of life, including all the noise and activity that seems to surround us continually, can erode our core: who we are, what we are, what we do, and what we're moving forward toward. These are distractions that can increasingly eat away at our beliefs and values, subtly and over time, until we become a shadow or a memory of what we wanted to be, to do, to become.

Get Back on Track

Quiet time gives us an opportunity to examine and to evaluate where we are in relationship to the core of what is most important to us in our lives. We can often find, with quiet time, where we've gotten off track, as well as what we need to do to get back on track, with the things that really matter most about us and our lives: character, authenticity, integrity, consistency, and trustworthiness.

Without quiet time, we will eventually wander so far off course of what we want to be and what we intended to be that a return to that will be difficult, if not impossible (once the vision is lost, it is no longer relevant and, with time, will not even be a part of who we are).

Quiet time also gives us a chance to charge ourselves. The human body, mind, and soul is like a battery - the more it's used, the more run down it becomes. If there are not regular intervals of recharging, then the body, the mind, the soul wear down and wear out. There are no replacements for these once they are worn down and worn out in this physical life.

So, my fellow quintessential leaders, with regard to regular intervals of quiet time in our lives, how are we doing?

Chapter 5: Ensure That You and Your Life Match Your Words

(I wrote this on July 4, 2014, the 238th anniversary of the signing of the Declaration of Independence in the United States.)

This Declaration of Independence, signed on July 4, 1776, formalized the intent of the colonies in the United States to sever themselves from British rule and become an independent nation with an independent government.

While in the United States this anniversary has mainly devolved into a day off of work, cookouts, and fireworks with little thought or attention given to the words it memorializes, it seems appropriate today to look at the some of the key words of that document and measure them against the lives of and the people who signed it to see if they match up.

This is the tough stuff of quintessential leadership. Many people can say - or write - noble, lofty, eloquent, and morally-upright words. However, the reality is that few of them and their lives match those words.

Let's look at a very prominent example (there are many) from the American Declaration of Independence and the signers and their lives.

"We hold these truths to be self-evident, that all men are created equal, that they are endowed by their Creator with certain unalienable Rights, that among these are Life, Liberty and the pursuit of Happiness." Almost every American knows these famous words written by Thomas Jefferson near the beginning of the Declaration of Independence and to which he and 55 other men affixed their signatures of belief and agreement.

But did they and their lives match them?

The answer is "no." Let's examine why.

"...all men are created equal..." is the place to start. This document was written in a time when "men" was a synonym for "humanity," or as the document says "mankind." Therefore, the words *all men* apply to all people on the planet. In fact, this is the exact argument that Jefferson states for declaring independence from Britain.

However, in practice, neither Jefferson nor the other 55 signers of the Declaration of Independence and their lives matched these words. About 1/3 of the signers, including Jefferson, were slave owners.

Additionally, many of them supported (and some were involved personally in) the subsequent eradication of Native Americans from North America to expand the American land holdings on the continent.

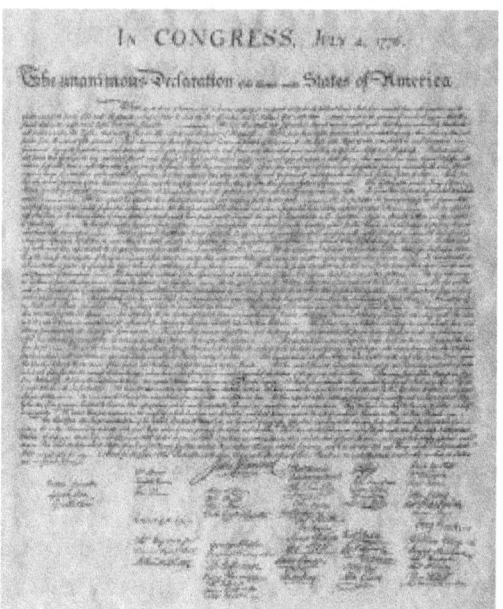

Here's where the rub comes in. Using a twisted take on the Bible, the signers rationalized the enslavement of Africans and the extermination of Native Americans. Because these two groups of people were not "Christians," they were considered sub-human, and therefore not "men" nor "mankind."

So, "all men" is disingenuous, because what it really means is all people who fit into a small set of criteria based on a self-determined (by Europeans and brought to America by the colonists) interpretation of the Bible.

Any person who did not meet the "all men" criteria, then, was not entitled to the "unalienable rights" of "Life, Liberty, and the pursuit of Happiness." And, sadly, this criteria has been the justification for wars, discrimination, and death ever since the signing of the Declaration of Independence on July 4, 1776.

So, what should we, as quintessential leaders, take away from this example?

The first thing is that when we and our lives don't match our words, we destroy trust and trustworthiness. Many of the signers of the Declaration of Independence became idolized and sanitized paragons of virtue and trustworthiness in the first 200 years or so after the Declaration was signed. For United States children, these myths were taught to us as American history.

However, in the last several decades, the myths of the Founding Fathers have been dismantled with the good, the bad, and the ugly facts about them and their lives revealed, and, as Mark Antony says in his eulogy to Julius Caesar, "The evil that men do lives after them; the good is oft interred with their bones." The revelations about the Founding Fathers has destroyed the trustworthiness their myths presented them as having.

The second lesson is that our words must be transparent and they must mean what they say. In the case of the signers of the Declaration of Independence, their words appear to be all-inclusive of all humanity. In reality, they applied only to a specific group of people who met specific criteria.

The last lesson is that while we influence and persuade by our words, the real determinant of our character, integrity, and authenticity will be who we are and what our lives are. We must be in absolute sync with the words we say and write. Otherwise, we will be dishonest. And we will be hypocrites.

Matching who we are and our lives with our words is a continual challenge for quintessential leaders. It's not easy and we all fail from time to time. However, when we fail, we must take immediate action to correct it. And we must always be examining and comparing whether we and our lives match the words we say and write.

How are we doing?

Chapter 6: Understanding (and the Value of) Quiet Leaders

The difference between talkative people and quiet people is most often a temperament difference. Talkative people tend to be extroverts, while quiet people tend to be introverts. Talkative people process ideas by talking about them, while quiet people process ideas by thinking about them.

In terms of leadership, at least in the western world, talkative people tend to be seen as strong leaders, while quiet people tend not to be seen as leaders at all. Susan Cain does an excellent job of addressing this erroneous stereotyping in _Quiet: The Power of Introverts in a World That Can't Stop Talking_.

As a quintessential leader who is quiet, I find myself often in the minority among mostly talkative people: on my teams, in leadership positions, and in the general population. I tire of noise quickly and, in social situations, being around very talkative people for long periods of time tends to wear me out. But long before I'm worn out, I've shut down and stopped listening.

However, in my leadership roles, I can't afford to shut down and stop listening, so I've had to learn how to lead talkative people - who sometimes have really great ideas and input somewhere in all the circuitous ways they express them - so that they can contribute their talent and assets in a meaningful way that works well for everybody involved:

> - Give them a time limit. Talkative people have no concept of time and will talk as long as they think someone is listening. Giving them a time limit - mine is 5 minutes - and sticking to it leads them, eventually, to being prepared, concise, and to the point if they want their ideas and input considered. It won't happen the first time. But each time talkative people are cut off by the time limit imposed will reinforce the fact that they need to be concise to be heard.
> - Lead them to "cut to the chase." This means asking them to give a conclusion when they start giving explanations. Ask questions about outcomes (what, when, and where) - instead of processes (why and how). Talkative people need a lot of redirecting to stay on track, and quintessential leaders care enough about their teams to invest the time to redirect. Even if it drives us quiet leaders a bit crazy in the process. :-)

For talkative people and talkative quintessential leaders, dealing with quiet people and quiet quintessential leaders can be challenging.

Talkative people and quintessential leaders think, speak, and commit quickly. And since they see this as a strength, they believe that everyone else should too. Quiet people and quintessential leaders will take or ask for time before they speak or commit.

And here's the big-picture advantage of that. Talkative says "let's just get it done and move on." Quiet says "let's take the time to do it right."

Talkative people and quintessential leaders get things done very quickly, but when they've moved on to other new and exciting things, a team is left behind fixing problems, mistakes, and issues that were not addressed because there was no upfront planning and analysis done.

A real-world example of this is Microsoft. The company has never released a product that didn't have major flaws and issues that required tons of patches and fixes after the release. My general rule of thumb is to avoid any Microsoft product update for at least a year, because that's usually how long it takes for the company to get a halfway stable version.

Quiet people and quintessential leaders commit slowly, but they stick with their commitments through thick and thin. Once they've made a commitment, they will see it through to a successful end. (Talkative people tend to commit quickly, but they also tend to drop out quickly when something new catches their attention.)

So how can talkative and quiet people and quintessential leaders form successful teams and partnerships? Here are some tips for the talkers (inherent in these is the value that quiet brings to the table) when working with those of us who are quiet:

> Don't mistake our silence - or even our seeming lack of reaction - for disinterest or disengagement or consent or rejection. We are thinking extensively in a detailed, systematic, and analytical way that you'll really appreciate if we decide to commit later.
> When you've finished your pitch, stop talking and embrace silence, no matter how uncomfortable it makes you. When you keep talking after you've done your presentation to those of us who are quiet, it (a) interrupts thinking; (b) comes across as putting pressure on us and rushing us into decision-making; and (c) makes it more likely that we will pass on being a part of the team/project/partnership.
> Tell those of us who are quiet why our participation is important. Since we make investments when we commit, the issue of importance is critical. Don't be surprised, though, if you and we see "important" differently. For talkers, almost everything tends to be important in the moment. Those of us who

are quiet, however, tend to see big-picture and long-term things as being really important. So if there's not a mesh of "important," we won't participate or commit.

- ➤ Don't keep asking those of us who are quiet what we are thinking. If we weren't quiet, we'd be monologue-style telling you to the point of boredom. When we're done thinking, we'll let you know in a very concise, fully-edited summary.
- ➤ Respect our space. Quiet people tend to have a bigger need for space than talkative people. In fact, talkative people often don't have any concept of space. Their way of connecting to other people is to get closer in proximity and to get louder in tone. Nothing drives those of us who are quiet away faster than this. Even if we were considering teaming or partnering with a talker, invasion of and obliviousness to our space will be the deal-breaker. Here's how to successfully navigate this: when and if we're ready, we will invite you into our space. But it takes time. So wait for the invitation instead of just barging in.

So, my fellow quintessential leaders, whether you are talkative or quiet, there's a way to successfully team and partner with each other and value what each type of quintessential leader brings to the table.

How are we doing?

Chapter 7: If Things Aren't Working, Then Change Them

Too often in life, we tend to settle for things that aren't working instead of taking the personal responsibility for changing them.

In tandem with this tendency, we also develop a <u>victim</u> mindset where we convince ourselves that the things we don't change are someone else's fault, someone else's responsibility to change, and someone else's problem to fix. This leads us to believe we don't have any control over things and it leads us to blame others when things aren't working instead of looking for solutions that we can take to change things.

One of the interesting side-effects of this victim mindset is the grumbling/mumbling/gossiping to others - the old adage of "misery loves company" in full swing - to try to form a victims' coalition where there's a lot of negative and nebulous talking about how things aren't working, but no positive and concrete action to initiate changes to make things work.

Quintessential leaders thoroughly understand the concept of personal responsibility. You will never find a victim mindset in a quintessential leader, no matter what circumstances he or she is in. Instead, quintessential leaders recognize that although they don't control everything that happens in their lives, there are things they have control over and can change.

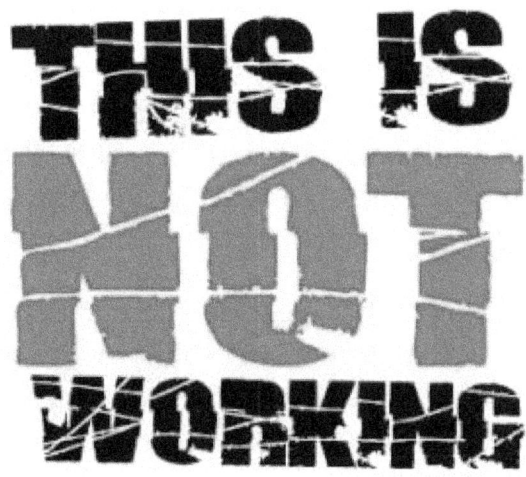

There is a logical sequence of realization, analysis, and implementation that quintessential leaders employ when things aren't working:

- ➢ What isn't working?
- ➢ Why isn't it working?
- ➢ What can I do to make it work?
- ➢ If I can't make it work in its current configuration, what changes can I make to the configuration to make it work?
- ➢ If the whole construct is faulty, what do I need to do to start over and make a new working construct?
- ➢ Take action!

In this systematic way of tackling things, large or small, that are not working lie some crucial differences between quintessential leaders and unquintessential leaders.

One difference is that quintessential leaders accept responsibility for changing what is not working within the scope of their abilities. Unquintessential leaders, however, wait for someone else to take the responsibility for change.

Ironically, it seems that most people don't realize that each of us has a large scope of ability in life to change the unworkable things that affect us. It is on a personal level that each of us has the greatest control. We may not always be able to change unworkable things on a large scale all the time, but we can always change how and what we do personally to make even the large-scale unworkable things work.

Another difference is that quintessential leaders are willing to risk failure to make the changes necessary when things aren't working. Unquintessential leaders are risk-adverse and fear failure more than anything else. As a result, unquintessential leaders will continue to accept things that are not working rather than facing the possibility of failure.

Here are some untold secrets about failure - if it happens (quintessential leaders have already **thought critically, deeply and analytically before they take action,** so the odds of failure are greatly diminished in most cases, but there are always factors out of our control that can bring failure no matter how well-designed and well-executed the plan is):

> ➢ It is not the end of the world.
> ➢ It is temporary.
> ➢ It is instructive.
> ➢ It produces resiliency.
> ➢ It sharpens commitment.
> ➢ It strengthens us.

A third difference is that quintessential leaders will persevere until they succeed to change things that aren't working into things that are working, no matter how much time, effort, and energy they are required to invest.

Unquintessential leaders, on the other hand, either don't want to or don't have the patience to invest any more time, effort, or energy into things that aren't working than grumbling, mumbling, and gossiping about them takes.

So what things, my fellow quintessential leaders, in your lives aren't working? What are you doing about them? Are we following the road not generally taken and practically applying quintessential leadership to them or is this an area of life where we are practicing unquintessential leadership?

No matter where we are right now in this area of life, it's never too late to change. Today is a good day to begin that change to practical application of quintessential leadership.

Above all, we must always be consciously aware that what we choose to do not only affects us, but also leaves a legacy as it teaches and sets an example for the family, social, educational, and organizational teams within our spheres of influence.

How are we doing?

Chapter 8: Thinking Critically, Deeply, and Analytically, Then Doing

This "this-is-what-it-looks-like" attribute of quintessential leadership practically applied has been on my mind for several months. In other words, I've been thinking critically and deeply about it and that has led to me writing this.

As a quintessential leader who thinks critically, deeply, and analytically about things before committing to executing them or abandoning them completely before execution - or if they're not working despite good thinking, during execution - I am aware that this method is the exception to the rule in general in most organizations.

And these organizations look busy with team members working from early morning to late at night, but the actual accomplishment and productivity - and profitability - is miniscule compared to the time and effort put in.

Why?

The reasons are multifaceted and too complex to break down into a simple bullet list, but two reasons stand out prominently.

One reason is that our society has developed a short-term and in-the-moment mentality that has resulted in the belief that simply doing something is what is important.

Whether that "something" should be done, whether it's worthwhile to do, whether it has long-term value, or whether it will accomplish something meaningful and beneficial is rarely, if ever, considered.

We, as a society, place a high value on how "busy" we are instead of whether all these things keeping us crazy busy are moving us and those around us forward for the better or we're just killing time and making a really good - but totally meaningless in the long run - show of it.

Most people in leadership positions, in all organizations, - as well as their teams - have this busy=accomplishment-and-productivity mindset, where down time is associated with stagnation and a lack of productivity and progress.

But down time is the key ingredient missing from most organizational constructs. Not only does down time give room for thinking critically, deeply, and analytically before embarking on new initiatives, but it also recharges the mental and physical batteries, so to speak, to actually accomplish those initiatives that progress forward from the thinking process to the execution process.

In business terms, this is the strategic phase of planning. However, regardless of the lip service that almost every organization gives to strategic planning, in actuality very little of it occurs.

As Mike Myatt points out in his blog post "Leaders Who Think More - Accomplish More", "Most businesses have devolved into an execution culture where getting things done is valued above all else. Too many companies wrongly confuse a strong work ethic and "getting stuff done" with accomplishing the right outcomes - they are not always one in the same. Doing for the sake of doing just adds to the noise and creates more chaos. By contrast good leadership (and good thinking) quiets the noise by providing great clarity."

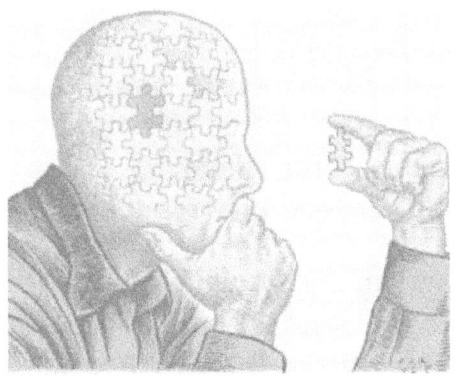

The crux of the problem is with the actual ability, desire, and discipline to think critically, deeply, and analytically before doing. Because society values impulsiveness, multitasking, and jumping from one thing to another in the blink of an eye, society has lost the ability, the desire, and the discipline to stop and take time to think things through from beginning to end before taking action.

Society has also lost the ability to stop, take in, and digest complex and serious ideas and information altogether. It takes too much time. It takes too much effort. It makes our eyes glaze over.

Society has been hookwinked by and trapped into a sound byte way of receiving and processing information. It is from those sound bytes that we fool ourselves into thinking we're informed, educated, and know all there is to know about any subject (which feeds directly into being "busy," being impulsive, multitasking, and jumping from one thing to another), when in reality we are just as, if not more, uninformed, uneducated, and ignorant as we were before we heard or read the sound byte.

As a blogger and an author who, along with a small minority of bloggers and authors in the worldwide landscape of the written word, writes substantively, seriously, and concretely, I see this played out over and over day in and day out, especially in the social media landscape where junk abounds and flourishes and most participants (especially bloggers who simply reblog or put a bunch of useless and mindless content out every day to trick the search engines into thinking they're "busy" posting a lot) aren't even capable of original content.

The more unimportant, the more ignorant, the more mindless, the more silly, the more profane, the more insulting, the more ridiculous, the more inane something is, the more it appears on all the social media platforms and the more wholesale approval it gets.

On the other hand, the more serious, the more substantive, the more important something is, the more likely it is to be ignored altogether.

The bottom line? In short, we, as a society, hate, reject and don't want our lives filled with substance, seriousness, and information that requires us to think, while we, as a society, love, embrace, and want our lives filled with drivel and garbage and information that doesn't require us to think.

As a quintessential leader, this trend - which mirrors the organizational trend - causes great consternation for me. The question I ask myself continually is "what happens if nobody knows how to think critically, deeply, and analytically anymore?"

That scenario is not something I want to be a part of, although the possibility of that grows more and more probable each day. Much like Winston Smith in George Orwell's 1984, I can envision being, if not completely alone, in a shrinking minority of the human race who embraces critical, deep, and analytical thought, absolute truth, and substance that matters.

As quintessential leaders, we must be diligent to eschew the tide of societal and organizational trends that value execution without thinking first, as well as the banal, the profane, the ridiculous, the ignorant, the unimportant, and being busy just for the sake of being busy. This is a colossal waste of our time, our energy, and our effort.

Instead we must be willing to think before we do, determining before we ever start on the execution phase of everything we undertake whether it's valuable, whether it's worthwhile, whether it's meaningful, and whether it has and will produce progress and long-term benefits for all who will be impacted by it.

If we take this step first, we will ensure that our time, energy, and our effort, as well as the time, energy, and effort expended by our teams, is used wisely, efficiently, and effectively and provides the maximum benefit to the most people.

The challenge I leave with you, my fellow quintessential leaders, is to determine whether you've abandoned critical, deep, and analytical thinking in favor of just being busy and accomplishing little or nothing of substance or value or whether you're taking this necessary first step and applying it to everything in your life before you undertake it.

I do it every day. I can answer this for myself only. You can answer for yourself only.

How are we doing?

Chapter 9: A Page From My Life

I signed a contract recently for the sale of my condo. Because I had to be moved out by within six weeks, I sat down and made a master list of things, in order of priority, that need to be done in the next month to accomplish the move.

The first thing on my list was to get quotes from moving companies with the plan being to finalize a choice on Tuesday of next week after I had a chance to compare the quotes, services, etc. and have a little time to think it over.

My first quintessential leader action was to involve my moving team. Since my mind has been overwired and overtaxed with all the stuff that needs to be done - and I will, because of circumstances, have to handle a lot of this alone - I asked one of my team members to send me a list of questions/things that I needed to talk with the moving companies about so that I wouldn't miss anything because of the mental overload in formulating an organized and executable plan.

With that list, I was able to more easily spend the majority of the first day of planning on the phone talking to potential moving companies.

I know talking on the phone is one of my areas of weakness because of the time it takes for me to process what I hear verbally with no visual aids to make any kind of cogent sense out of it.

I prefer to get information in writing, because reading is my strength when it comes to immediate understanding, comprehension, and decision-making. I can very quickly get through all the extraneous stuff and cut to the chase when I'm reading.

However, when someone's talking to me (and this gets compounded exponentially when I can't read body language and facial expressions), I'm filtering, trying to figure out what's salient, trying to put that in writing, and trying to remember everything I need to say or ask. It's a very grueling task for me and I don't enjoy it and actively try to avoid it as much as possible.

So, mindful of that weakness, I had my list of things to ask about and discuss and I finished each phone call with a request for the things we discussed to be emailed to me in a finalized quote, just in case I hadn't gotten everything written down in the notes I'd taken during our conversations.

There were also some quintessential leadership lessons from the various moving companies I talked with. I'm always surprised - although I shouldn't be - at how much unquintessential leadership exists today, but I got a strong reminder of it yesterday.

I was also acutely aware of <u>the traits that build trust and make us trustworthy</u> and of their general absence in society today, including organizationally.

Almost as soon as I'd put in a request for quotes, my phone rang with the first moving company.

One thing I noticed about the owner was that he didn't ask me the right questions. Another thing I noticed was that when I asked questions, he was either overly agreeable or he wouldn't answer me directly.

Of course, I kept coming back to those questions because I wasn't comfortable with his answers, and I got the same kinds of responses. That put me on high alert almost right away.

The last thing that he did was to try to manipulate me into making a decision yesterday, both on the phone and in the written quote that he sent me, although I told him up front that I was talking with several companies and wouldn't make a decision until I'd done my research.

After I got off the phone with him, I did a complaint search on his company and the number of and kind of complaints were the very things I had asked him about and he was evasive about.

The quintessential leader practical application lesson? Dishonesty, evasiveness, and manipulation (these were all issues in every single complaint about the company) are unquintessential leader traits and they will destroy an organization, no matter how compelling the sales pitch may seem. Although his company offered the lowest quote, once I was armed with information, I understood why and crossed the company off my list.

I had one other company contact me by phone, but I had to initiate the call with the other three.

One of the companies I called didn't have anyone answering the phones, so I crossed it off the list. Unquintessential leadership is being unresponsive.

The owner of another company answered the phone after a few rings and I couldn't believe this owner was still even in business. I told him the information about the move and asked him if he could give me a quote. His response was that I needed to send him an email that detailed everything I needed to move and he'd see if he was able to get me a quote.

I crossed his company off the list. Unquintessential leadership is making your customers, whom you serve, do all the work and then expecting them to give their business and money to you.

The other company that contacted me by phone made some of the same mistakes that the first company that contacted me by phone made. Although the quote was higher than the first company's quote, the owner was just as evasive in answering some of the questions that I asked, even though I asked them several times to try to nail down details.

One of the real red flags was that this company gave estimates based on an guessed-at calculated weight based on my description of what was being moved, and that could, to quote the owner, "go up or down, depending on the actual weight." This was the only company that couldn't give me a locked-in price, and I could see the potential disaster in that scenario right off the bat.

Additionally, like the first company I talked with, the owner tried to pressure me into making a decision right then, using the same manipulative techniques that the first company owner used. When I told him I was still in the research phase, he actually got irritated and told me that if I didn't get something in place with his company by the end of yesterday, then I had "a snowball's chance in hell" of getting moved on my timeline.

Integrity

I was so appalled talking with this owner on the phone that I actually marked his company off the list while I was still on the phone with him.

The unquintessential leadership was everywhere in this conversation and with this owner. The guesswork involved in the weight estimate, the lack of a locked-in price, and the owner's irritation and subsequent pronouncement on the chances of my move being successful in my time frame were just a few examples of his unquintessential leadership.

The final company I contacted was different. They had sent me an email with a link to their site and I went through the site thoroughly before calling them.

I noticed they had an A+ rating with the Better Business Bureau with no complaints in the last year and they were listed with Angie's List with an A rating as well. They also had fantastic customer reviews, including a couple from state historical sites who raved about the excellent care and professionalism used in moving things that were worth a lot of money.

I called them and, although I did not talk with the owner, I did talk with the person in charge of setting up interstate moves.

I began by asking my questions. Not only did this person answer them directly, but he gave me additional information on how this moving company differed from most moving companies in their staff, what they offered that other moving companies didn't offer, and how they handled transactions differently from other moving companies.

He also explained to me that if I could give him a window of time for the move as opposed to an exact date, it would give him an opportunity to look for discounts and give me the best locked-in price possible.

Unlike all the other companies I spoke with, he did not give me a quote over the phone, but instead he asked for time to work on a written quote which he would email to me.

It was refreshing change of pace after what I'd spent most of the rest of the day dealing with because quintessential leadership was in full evidence.

The person I spoke with was responsive, non-evasive, non-manipulative, and actually proactively gave me some very good advice and guidance on what the moving industry does in general and what to look for and what to avoid when dealing with moving companies. Additionally, he didn't try to high-pressure me into a "done deal" yesterday, but instead asked for me to give him time to get the best possible time/price for my move.

We have many opportunities every day in the pages of our lives to be quintessential leaders. Whether we are or not is evident in who and how we are, what we do, what we say, and how we do what we do and how we say what we say. Quintessential leadership is not something we put on and take off at will. It is who we are all the time.

Similarly, we have many opportunities to observe the presence or absence of quintessential leadership in our daily activities. These are instructive and we can learn a lot about what and how we need to do and be and what and how we don't want to do and be.

So the questions we need to ask and answer throughout each day are quite simple.

"Am I consistently a quintessential leader during this page of my life?" is the first question. The answers will tell us what we need to change, improve, and/or replace in our lives.

The second question is "were the people my life intersected with today quintessential leaders or not?" The answers to this question make us think more deeply about what quintessential leadership is and isn't.

Additionally, they remind us to look into the mirrors of our own lives to see if we see reflections of quintessential leadership or unquintessential leadership, because it's often when we are observers of and recipients of the actions of others that we become more acutely aware of the good, the bad, and the ugly in ourselves.

And that promotes growth and change in us as quintessential leaders, which, after all, is the goal we're all striving for.

Let's not miss the every-day opportunities we have to become better quintessential leaders than we were yesterday. They're all around us, even in the most mundane of things, but we have to be attuned to them so they don't slip by us and we miss them.

How are we doing?

Chapter 10: Personal Accountability and Personal Responsibility

Dan Rockwell's blog post entitled "Five Ways Bad Bosses Make You Look Bad" capped off one of several things I've been mulling over the last few weeks and it provided me with the finishing touch I needed for this chapter.

Rockwell accurately states that when we resort to complaining about other people - in leadership positions or not - we automatically give those people control of our attitudes, speech, behaviors, contributions, and futures.

What does this look like? In short, we take a reactive position based on what someone else is doing - or not doing - and that takes up all our time, energy, actions, and thinking.

It also negates our personal accountability and personal responsibility for what we do and who we are because we're resorting to putting all the responsibility on someone else to make things acceptable to and for us.

I heard a sermon once where the pastor referred to this very behavior as "riding in the back seat of your life" (as opposed to driving the car) and that phrase has stuck with me as I work to become a better quintessential leader and a better human being, and I hope it sticks with all of you as well.

Because that's exactly what we do when we give up or hand over our personal accountability and personal responsibility to someone else.

How do we, as quintessential leaders, combat this? Here are a few lessons I've learned along the way.

Complaining is just complaining. It never changes anything - or anyone - for the better. The only results of complaining are changes in those of us who are complaining for the worse: bitterness, resentment, anger, hate, frustration, and capitulation (giving up).

We will never and do not have the ability to change anyone else. The only people we can and have the ability to change are ourselves.

We all have people in our lives, whether they are in leadership positions or not, that fit the "bad boss" description.

However, we are not personally accountable nor personally responsible for their changes. On the other hand, we are personally accountable and personally responsible for our changes.

And we are not taking that personal accountability and responsibility for ourselves and what we can and need to do in our own lives to change if all we are doing is giving detailed dissertations about how and what other people need to change and/or trying to sabotage and thwart them at every turn to try to force them to change.

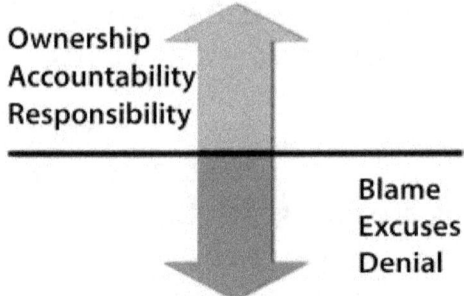

Ownership
Accountability
Responsibility

Blame
Excuses
Denial

It's a waste of time, of energy, and of opportunities for us to proactively change what we can to make ourselves and our lives better.

Rockwell includes a list in his blog post about how to be proactive (taking personal accountability and personal responsibility for ourselves) in "bad boss" relationships.

This list includes things that enable us to let the "bad boss" people in our lives bring out our best instead of letting them bring out our worst.

Forgiveness is listed near the bottom of Rockwell's list. However, as quintessential leaders, forgiveness should be at the top of our lists.

Because everything else on the list depends upon forgiveness being extended first.

Forgiveness is perhaps one of the hardest things that we human beings are called upon to do. It is extremely difficult when there's real and legitimate pain, real and legitimate mistreatment, real and legitimate hurt.

But forgiveness also calls upon the quality of our character: who *are* we as people? Do we sink to the lowest common denominator of a contentious, vengeful, unforgiving society and world around us? Do we sink to the level of the people who wrong us (intentionally or unintentionally)?

Or do we rise above our emotional, mental, and physical hurt and pain to extend the same forgiveness and mercy that we often find we need to have extended to us as well?

Forgiveness is the first act of personal accountability and personal responsibility. It literally requires that we initiate the process without knowing or expecting that anything will necessarily change on another person's part.

I will also say that forgiveness, especially when the hurt and the pain is deep, is not just the act of saying "I forgive you." The heart and the emotions and the mind sometimes take a much longer time to catch up with the words.

But the words state our intent, and once that intent is stated, we are committed to diligently complete that course of action, no matter how long it takes for all of what makes us human to get in sync and make it a total reality.

At the end of this gig called life, there are only a handful of things that actually matter: how much we grew up as people, the depth of our character, and whether we persevered in integrity - perseverance alone is not enough - to the end of the marathon, or we mistakenly believed that this gig was just a few short sprints and we quit running altogether because we got tired or we decided it wasn't worth the effort.

And the state and quality of that handful of things, my fellow quintessential leaders, is directly tied to how much personal accountability and personal responsibility we take in each of own our lives.

How are we doing?

Chapter 11: Navigating Rough Seas in Relationships

As long as there are humans, there will be rough seas from time to time in our relationships. Rough seas, however, are one of the areas in which quintessential leadership - or the lack of it - will be very evident.

How we respond to the rough seas in our relationships says a lot about who we are as people and as leaders. It also says a lot about the value we put on our relationships.

But, most importantly, how we respond to the rough seas reveals the quality of our character and whether we are truly striving to be quintessential leaders or just giving the effort lip service.

There are some things in life that can obviously cause rough seas in relationships: miscommunication, misunderstandings, unintentional hurts, and perceptions of betrayal (I say perception here because I'm not talking about actual betrayal, which ends relationships, but an unfounded and untrue presumption of betrayal by one or the other person in a relationship).

These require immediate action and rectification and quintessential leaders will do that. Often, quintessential leaders will anticipate that these may have occurred before there is any evidence of a problem and work to fix and restore the relationship to good standing before rough seas materialize.

However, there are some very subtle things that can cause rough seas in relationships, and those are often the product of, often through no fault of the person in the relationship going through it, prolonged internal upheaval that spills out and into the spaces of their relationships.

And this is where quintessential leaders stand out from everyone else in how they handle these rough seas in

their relationships.

They show their character, their integrity, their trustworthiness and their commitment to the relationships, in their lives, and in who they are when the rough seas in their relationships materialize.

Quintessential leaders take their relationships seriously. They are invested in them for the long haul without conditions related to the tenor of the relationships at any given time.

Quintessential leaders understand that life is not all peaches and cream. They also understand that relationships will have rough seas when life throws curve balls at the people involved.

And quintessential leaders understand that the rough seas are when they are needed most and can do the most to ensure that the relationship not only stays intact, but is fortified and strengthened.

It's not always easy, it's not always pleasant, and it's definitely not always fun, but quintessential leaders know it's always necessary if they truly value and care about the relationships and the people involved.

So, what does quintessential leader handling of rough seas in relationships look like in practice? Let's find out.

Quintessential leaders stay *actively engaged* in the relationship, and, in fact, will often increase their engagement during rough seas. In other words, they endure through good times, bad times, sad times, and in-between times.

For some people, it might be easier to turn away and find relationships that don't present - at least now - many rough seas to deal with and that are easy on the mind, the heart, and the soul for the most part. In the fickle way that society views, treats, and establishes relationships now, that's generally what most people opt for.

Quintessential leaders don't, though. They've been through enough of their own rough seas in relationships that they have experienced that sense of total abandonment, and they are committed to not being the source of abandonment in their own relationships where other people have hit rough seas.

Quintessential leaders *listen*. And listen. And listen. But not only do quintessential leaders listen, they also hear and look for what is really going on behind the words they hear, many of which may just be raw, unfiltered, from-the-heart thinking that the person saying them is entrusting them with.

It can be very difficult to listen to extremely intense and painful thoughts and feelings. It can be even more difficult to keep listening as intensity and pain, which ebb and flow just like any other kind of thinking and feeling, sometimes crescendo into a temporary deluge all at once.

At this rough sea in our relationships, quintessential leaders distinguish themselves by recognizing that a temporary line of thinking doesn't define the other person in that person's totality, but instead shows that we're all weak, vulnerable, and scared sometimes, and those weaknesses, vulnerabilities, and fears come to the surface occasionally when we're in crises.

Quintessential leaders don't define people by one or more temporary situations. Instead, they recognize, through listening, all the factors in play that lead to these temporary situations, compare those with these same people in their totality, and instead of cutting people off, disconnecting, or simply abandoning them, quintessential leaders respond by continuing to listen.

Quintessential leaders, in response to hearing, will continually and proactively
offer *support, encouragement, empathy*,
and *compassion* during the rough seas in their
relationships.

They understand that it might not always be acknowledged or even, at that moment, accepted, but quintessential leaders also know those who are on the receiving end will appreciate it and be grateful for it.

This, by the way, does not come in the form of trite expressions ("don't worry," "everything will be fine," etc.) or dismissive comments ("you don't really believe that, do you?," "I can't believe you're thinking that way," "you know that's not true," etc.), which often can make things worse.

Instead, quintessential leaders express it in a well-thought-out and well-expressed acknowledgement that they've heard and they understand, but they also know the bigger picture of the people in the relationships and are persistent about focusing on and expressing that.

That's a very big deal - more probably than any of us actually realize -when there are rough seas in relationships, and it's hard sometimes both on the giving and receiving end to do, but quintessential leaders know and understand that it's essential and it matters.

Another practical way that quintessential leaders handle rough seas in relationships is by showing *kindness* and *gentleness*, whether they're the one in the rough seas or somebody else is.

One of the characteristics that sets quintessential leaders apart is the objective ability to move from walking in their own shoes and seeing through their own eyes into walking in the shoes and seeing through the eyes of others.

Quintessential leaders are continually seeking, through listening, through observation, and through engagement, to understand others, especially everyone they have relationships with.

Most people don't know how to walk in someone else's shoes and see through someone else's eyes, because we're not really taught to do that in life and it's unnatural and extremely tough to move our feet and eyes from our egocentric view of everything and actually try to understand and see from another perspective.

Although the ability to do this doesn't come naturally to most people, it can be learned. For some of us, it comes naturally, and for some of us, it was worth it to learn how to do it. Most people, however, have simply never even thought about, and, therefore, don't do it.

Even most of the minority who do try to walk in other's shoes and see through others' eyes don't do it consistently or well (making assumptions, which more often than not are inaccurate and wrong, are frequently mistaken for putting ourselves in others' shoes).

Quintessential leaders don't make assumptions. They literally - and this is because they know and understand the people in their relationships well because they are important to them - move away from how they view things and consider how the others involved view them, as well as considering everything else going on in the lives of those others.

So when rough seas in relationships occur, quintessential leaders are naturally able to be gentle and kind because they can "see" how the rough seas are affecting the others involved.

This attribute makes quintessential leaders tend to be very merciful toward others, both within their relationships and within humanity in general.

Instead of getting upset and angry at others - regardless of who's in the rough seas in the relationships - quintessential leaders keep the big picture in mind, not taking things personally, and granting a lot of latitude and eschewing outright rejection, veiled attacks, subtle put downs, and entrenched bitterness.

In short, quintessential leaders have developed - and continue to grow in - the ability to love at all times, to understand, as much as is humanly possible, all things, and to forgive (even though - and this is very rare, but it does happen - it make take considerable time, considerable space, and great, relentless effort), in the end, unconditionally.

This is because quintessential leaders are very invested in really knowing and understanding others.

Quintessential leaders generally default to giving everyone the benefit of the doubt. This doesn't mean that they're not constantly working (observation, research, proof) to remove the "doubt" one way or the other, but they generally give people an unfettered chance to prove themselves on their own merit.

Quintessential leaders, therefore, realize that whatever's happening in the rough seas of their relationships is probably not conscious, nor intentional, nor malicious. It's just, unfortunately, a more common than uncommon human foible.

So the question I leave you with is: are you a quintessential leader when your relationships have rough seas in them?

Chapter 12: Do You Stoke the Fire or Calm the Flames?

One of the most difficult areas that people in leadership positions have to deal with is tensions and conflicts between other people.

Unquintessential leaders often tend to take one of two extreme approaches. One is to ignore the situation and pretend it doesn't exist. The other is threaten drastic action if the tensions and conflicts don't cease and desist.

Neither of these is effective and, in fact, both are quite damaging and destructive to teams and to organizations. Why? Because the issues that are causing the conflicts and tensions are not being addressed.

But the worst thing that people in leadership positions - and I have seen this way too many times to think it's an aberration - can do with conflicts and tensions between other people is to stoke the fire.

This is done by encouraging the tensions and conflicts - and often contributing to the increased conflagration by getting involved on one side or the other and sometimes both sides because they're enjoying the show - until the conflicts and tensions become an all-out war that threatens to obliterate the entire team (and, eventually, the organization).

This is unquintessential leadership at its absolute worst.

On the other hand, though, handling tensions and conflicts is how quintessential leaders demonstrate what quintessential leadership looks like in practice.

How?

Quintessential leaders create an environment where disrespect is not an option. They recognize that tension and conflict are inevitable in human relationships - sometimes because of personalities and temperament and sometimes because there is a legitimate disagreement - but quintessential leaders set the standards for how people treat each other and how conflicts are resolved and tensions eliminated.

Quintessential leaders, therefore, are proactive about resolving conflicts and tensions as soon as they materialize. In general, quintessential leaders take the following steps to mediate - key word (not fix) - resolution.

Quintessential leaders get everyone involved together (outside of the organizational setting is best) and set out to find out what's behind the conflict or tension. Often this is the simplest way and fastest route to resolution because each person has the opportunity, respectfully, to talk and to be heard.

After listening to everyone (and ascertaining the root cause or issue), quintessential leaders then ask each person how committed, on a numerical scale (1-5 is what I normally use), he or she is to resolution.

For any participant in this discussion whose number is lower than the top number of the scale, quintessential leaders then ask why his or her commitment is lower. These have to be quantifiable reasons ("just because" or "I don't like..." is not good enough).

Most conflicts and tensions have a strong emotionally-based component that obscures the actual issue that needs to be addressed, but when pressed to quantify emotions, those involved in the conflict or tension will be able to see that their involvement is primarily an emotional and subjective reaction instead of a logical, objective reaction.

Once the emotions are out of the way, then resolving the actual point of contention is possible. Quintessential leaders guide this process, but they don't offer the fix. Instead, they lead those involved to find the fix, within the established team and organizational parameters, that they can all agree upon among themselves.

And here's a key reason why quintessential leaders are quintessential leaders.

They understand that they have the power to legislate and enforce their solutions on the process. In fact, that's, from a logical standpoint, the shortest distance between A and B.

However, quintessential leaders understand that, in the big picture, this ends up being detrimental to each person, the team, and the organization for these reasons:

1. Legislated and enforced solutions don't get buy-in and usually create even more conflict and tension.
2. By participating in the process of learning how to resolve conflicts and tensions with others, each individual learns life skills that enable them to both be less likely to get embroiled in future conflicts and tensions and be better able, if they do find themselves in that situation, to resolve them sooner and without outside intervention.
3. Quintessential leaders are developed by concretely practicing and applying

quintessential leadership. That's impossible for them to do if someone else is always fixing things for them and not letting them do the actual work and build these habits themselves.

So my question to you, my fellow quintessential leaders, is, when conflict and tensions arise, do you stoke the fire or calm the flames?

Addendum: Other Books (Available on Amazon in Paperback and Kindle Format) by The Quintessential Leader

Building Trust and Being Trustworthy

Qualities of Quintessential Leaders